C000138087

Things I Can't Explain

I Know in My Heart, God Played a Part

Lucy Geddes

Peter E. Randall Publisher
Portsmouth, New Hampshire
2024

Peter E. Randall Publisher
5 Greenleaf Woods Drive, Suite 102
Portsmouth, NH 03801
www.perpublisher.com

Library of Congress Control Number: 2024902655

ISBNs: 979-8-9902484-0-3 softcover; 979-8-9902484-1-0 hardcover

Printed in the United States of America

Dedication

To my wonderful husband, Ken, who has always believed in me and supported me in so many ways, especially with technology!

To my mother, Rachel, and my grandmother, Doria, whose love and support was the foundation of my life. The way they lived their lives taught me how to live mine.

To my dad, Jerry, who was always there for me and all of his family.

Contents

Preface

This book is a spiritual autobiography of events that have occurred in my life. I don't know why these events (premonitions and so forth) happen to me, or when they will happen. I have decided to name it a "sixth sense." I think everyone has this sixth sense, but some people may be more aware of it than others. I recognize it in the stories that other people have shared with me about their spiritual experiences.

God has been encouraging me to write and share these experiences with others. I don't know why. Maybe it's so others will recognize their spiritual experiences or where God plays a part in their lives. I know there are many times when I don't recognize how He has played a part or helped me until much later. Whatever the reason, I hope that this book helps you in some way.

Chapter 1

How Did I Know?

One day while at work, I got a call from my Aunt Claire, saying that my grandmother, Doria, wasn't feeling well. I told her that when I left school, I would drive over to see her. When I got to my grandmother's house, my aunt and her daughter Linda (my older cousin) were sitting by my grandmother's bed talking to her. My dad, Gerald—or Jerry, which is what most people called him— was also there. My parents lived upstairs, but my mother, Rachel, who usually looked after my grandmother, was away at the time.

When I walked into my grandmother's bedroom, she smiled at me, and we talked for a little while. I asked my aunt what her symptoms were, and she said my grandmother just didn't feel well. When I looked at my grandmother, she didn't look sick to me, but my grandmother never complained about anything.

We talked for a little while. When I eventually glanced at my watch, my aunt said, "You need to go home and make dinner for your three kids and your husband."

"I do, but maybe I should stay a little longer," I said.

My aunt assured me that my grandmother would be fine since she and my dad would be there, and said I should take care of my family. For some reason I didn't want to leave. However, my grandmother assured me she was fine. She smiled at me and said "I love you," softly. I told her I loved her, too, and I'd be back the next day to check on her. My grandmother and I were very close, as my family had always lived in my grandparents' house.

As I left, I thought, *She's always had problems with her blood pressure, so I should be used to this by now*. I decided to go home to take care of my family, make dinner, check on the kids regarding their activities and homework, and prepare for the next day.

When I got to school the next day, I reminded my paraprofessional, Nancy, that I had a dentist appointment at ten o'clock. I told her what I wanted her to teach our students for the rest of the day. I was confident that she was capable of taking over for me because we had worked together so well for many years.

She looked at me and said, "I thought you'd only be gone an hour to an hour and a half?"

"Yes, I should be, but just in case I don't make it back today, I want you to know what to do with the students," I said.

"Why wouldn't you be coming back?" she asked.

"I don't know. I just have this feeling that I might not be," I replied.

Nancy looked at me strangely and said, "Okay." She knew that sometimes I had premonitions but that I didn't know what exactly they would be.

I went to my dentist appointment. Because I hadn't eaten breakfast, afterward I decided to go through the drive-through at Wendy's, but as I turned in, instead of going through the drive-through I went around the back and parked on the side. It was as if my car had a mind of its own. I sat there thinking, and then took out my phone and called my dad. No answer, but he could have been outside. I called my aunt. No answer, but they didn't have cell phones and probably didn't hear the phones ring inside the house.

I drove away from Wendy's and went straight to the emergency entrance at the hospital nearest to my grandmother's house. I was hoping that she wouldn't be there, but I had this feeling that she would be. I felt like I was being led there by God. After I parked my car, I walked in and gave my grandmother's name and asked if she had been brought there.

The nurse looked down at a paper, then looked up at me and asked, "How are you related to her?"

I said, "I'm her granddaughter."

She said, "Come with me."

She took me to a room where my dad and aunt were crying uncontrollably. My dad explained that when my aunt went to check on her the next morning, she was unresponsive. They had called 911. When the EMTs arrived, they administered CPR on her at home and in the ambulance, but they could not revive her. I started to cry, and I comforted both of them at the same time. I knew I had lost my best friend and confidante.

Finally, we regained some composure. The nurse asked if I wanted to see her, and I said yes. She asked me if I was sure, because my grandmother was still hooked up to a lot of tubes. I said yes, so my dad and my aunt and I went in together. I'm glad I did, but I will always remember her not in that moment, but as she is in the memories I have of her—the most wonderful grandma you could ever ask for. I feel that God led me to the hospital because my dad and aunt needed me there, and I also needed to see my grandmother one last time.

My grandmother was the person who had the most influence on my life, so I'd like to elaborate on what she was like and the ways she influenced me. I longed to be like her, as she always had a positive attitude and was very patient, encouraging, and complimentary to others, although she would correct any of her twenty-one grandchildren if the need arose.

I remember tiptoeing down the stairs on Saturday morning as a child to have coffee (more like milk with a little coffee in it) with her, as she always got up early. After school, sometimes I would ask her to tell me what it was like when she grew up. I loved to listen to her stories. It amazed me how much she had seen and lived through. She was born in 1901 and lived to be almost ninety-three years old. She lived through the Spanish Flu, World War I and World War II, the Depression, the loss of her first child at six or seven weeks old (who ironically had the same first name I have, even though my mother didn't know about my grandmother's first baby until after I was born), and so many other hardships. And yet, she was such a strong woman in her sweet, quiet, happy, kind, welcoming way to everyone.

My grandmother Doria never asked for anything but did so much for so many people. She was the ultimate community service volunteer. She was a midwife. I remember people coming to her door when she was older, people she knew from long ago who she had helped in some way or had been friends of her family.

I used to ask her to tell me what it was like long ago. One time she told me a story about how she would get up at four o'clock in the morning to make bread and wash her floors before the kids got up. She had seven children after her first child died. Because she had so many children, as a lot of people did at that time, she felt it was easier to do some of her chores before her children got out of bed. She lived on a farm at that time in her life so there were a lot of chores to be done.

She told me that at one point she had a neighbor whose wife had cancer. She told the neighbor to send his six or seven children over to her house for their meals and to send all their laundry with them (and she didn't have a washing machine like we have now and definitely no dryer, just clotheslines).

I was speechless as I listened intently to what she was telling me. I remember eventually saying to her, "How could you possibly feed thirteen or fourteen children and do all that laundry?!"

She looked at me, confused, and said, "That poor man had to take care of his wife and work. The least I could do was help him with his kids."

Wow! I thought. *Isn't that the way it should be? If someone needs help, you help if you can.*

In addition to all of the different ways she helped others, she also taught all of her grandchildren how to play cards as well as many of her great-grandchildren, which, I've been told, led to their above average mathematical skills.

My grandmother grew up in Montreal, Canada, but eventually most of her family (her parents, her two stepbrothers, and her) moved to New Hampshire. Her father started a barbershop business in Manchester. I remember my grandmother playing her piano at home, but she could only play by ear; she could not read music. When I was growing up my family would take trips to Montreal so my grandmother could visit with her sister, Irene, and Irene's family. When we were at her sister's house, Irene, who was a very good piano and organ player, would play a song so my grandmother could listen to the tune. Then the two of them would play together: Irene on her organ and my grandmother on Irene's piano.

My grandfather Joaquin (even though his name was Joaquin, everyone called him Jack) grew up in Madeira, Portugal. His father wanted him to have a better life and encouraged him to go to America. He immigrated to the United States on a sailing ship named *Madonna* when he was about twenty years old. I don't know his exact age, as my grandfather did not know the date of his birth, so when he arrived in the United States he chose a date: the Fourth of July. I don't know the exact year. He came through immigration in Providence, Rhode Island, on October 2, 1912. Sometime later, his father sent for him to return to Madeira to bring his younger brother Carlos (we knew him as Uncle Charlie) to America.

I don't know how they ended up in New Hampshire, but I do know that my grandfather got a job working in a textile mill, Chicopee Mills, in Manchester. He worked himself up to a weaver position, which requires a high skill level. After that he got a job spiking on the railroad. He also got my dad, Jerry, a job on the railroad so they worked together. On a side note, I found it very interesting that they were paid with silver dollars, some of which my grandfather would later give to his grandchildren. My father went from working on the railroad to the Army during World War II.

After my grandmother and grandfather met in New Hampshire (I don't know how they met, though I wish I did), they got married and started having babies. My grandfather's mother sent a beautiful, lacy white baby bonnet to them that my grandmother showed me one day when we were looking through her trunk in our attic. Many years later, after my parents passed away, I looked for that bonnet, but it was nowhere to be found.

I remember my grandmother telling me a story about how she almost met her father-in-law once. She and my grandfather had received a letter from her father-in-law telling them that he would be stopping in Boston and asking them if they could meet him there. He was a wine merchant who traveled by ship to different countries to sell his wine. My grandmother and grandfather took a train to Boston, but when they got there, they had a telegram waiting for them saying that the ship couldn't stop in Boston after all. I can't imagine how disappointing that must have been for them. My grandmother never got to meet her husband's family and my grandfather never got to see his parents and sister again. I think with bringing up seven children at that time, right after World War I, and working on a farm, they didn't have the monetary resources to travel to Madeira. To my knowledge her father-in-law never traveled to the United States again.

I look to my grandmother as a model of someone I strive to be. Even though she lived through so many difficult times, she was still a happy, optimistic, friendly, helpful, thoughtful, encouraging person up until the day she passed away. I look back and think of how lucky I was to have lived in the same house as my grandmother and grandfather.

Love you and miss you, Mémère and Pépère!

Chapter 2

Saying Goodbye

I have a cousin, Linda, who is like an older sister to me. We grew up two houses away from each other. She married a wonderful guy, Lucien. Even though he'd had a difficult childhood, Lucien was able to make a wonderful life for himself, his wife, Linda, and their daughter, Tracey.

When Linda and Lucien were growing up, their families lived in the same apartment building across the hall from each other. Because of this they got to know each other and enjoyed each other's company, although Lucien didn't have much free time. His parents had separated, and he and his younger brother, Tom, stayed with their father. Unfortunately, their father wasn't a good role model. Basically, Lucien was left to bring up his younger brother and do all the daily chores, including grocery shopping, cooking, laundry, cleaning, and attending school. When he graduated from high school he went into the Army. He and Linda also became engaged.

After Lucien's time in the Army, he and Linda got married. Lucien worked for Public Service of New Hampshire, a utility company, starting off as a meter reader and then becoming an electrician working on substations. He was on call to help with major power outages. These, of course, could happen any time of the day or night.

As busy as Lucien was, he always found time to coach his daughter Tracey's softball team and be there to cheer her on at her soccer games. He was very proud, as we all were, when Tracey graduated valedictorian of her class and went on to become a high school math teacher.

As they grew up, Tracey and our two boys, Derek and Brad, and our daughter, Melissa, enjoyed playing and spending time together. Our two families would do many things together, including taking vacations at the beach, going cross country skiing, and ringing in the New Year. Lucien was a happy, fun-loving guy who always had several jokes to tell. You could say he was the life of the party! He was also always ready to help anyone who needed help with anything, bringing along his tools if needed.

We were cross country skiing one winter day, when on the way home Lucien mentioned that he wasn't feeling well. We thought he might be getting a virus or a cold. However, when his symptoms continued to get worse, he went to see his doctor who scheduled some tests for him. The results showed he had cancer. While he was receiving treatment—a difficult time for him, his family, and his friends—I wondered why this was happening to him. He'd had such a difficult childhood and yet he had risen above that and made a good life for himself and his family and helped so many other people. Why did he have to have cancer? Why do bad things happen to good people? (Not that I wanted them to happen to anyone.) *Maybe someday we'll find out*, I thought.

Even though Lucien received treatment, he passed away that fall at a young age. About two days after he passed away, I was sitting in my classroom reading a story to my students. Suddenly, I felt his presence in my room. I turned to my left, where I felt his spirit. I felt like he was saying, "Oh, this is where you work, very nice." And then he was gone. This all happened in a matter of a few seconds. I turned to my class and continued the story. I thought about what had just happened for a long time. I wondered if he had visited others and maybe they weren't even aware of it. I can't help but wonder if his spirit was saying "Goodbye" before continuing on his journey. Even now it puts a smile on my face when I remember him "stopping by."

Lucien was loved by all who knew him, and we still miss him dearly. But in my heart, I'm happy that he is with God and living a Heavenly, cancer-free life. And we will meet again!

Chapter 3

The Big Dark Cloud

It was June 2001. My husband Ken and I were so excited to be celebrating our twenty-fifth wedding anniversary! It didn't seem real . . . how could we have been married for twenty-five years? But when we looked back at all that had happened in our lives, we knew it had to have been that long.

We started dating in February of our senior year in high school. We had both been working on our yearbook since the previous fall. Ken was the assistant make-up editor, and I was the copy editor and typing editor. Oddly enough we were both voted "Most Mature" by our class, and we weren't dating yet. We both went on to college after graduation. During the summer before junior year, Ken proposed to me. Two weeks after graduation we got married. We went on to have two sons, Derek and Brad, and a daughter, Melissa. We were involved in so many activities over twenty-five years—baseball, soccer, tennis, golf, Taekwondo, dance lessons, Girl Scouts, trumpet lessons, softball, camping vacations, Disney World, and so forth.

Now our sons were adults, and our daughter was a teenager. Our three children surprised us with a party, where we were so happy to see family and longtime friends; some of them had traveled quite far to be with us. We had so much fun at our party and then we were off on our first cruise to Bermuda! We had a wonderful time! So much so, that I didn't want to leave. But, of course, we did.

Over the course of the summer, I spent time with my mom. She had been wonderful to her children—loving, caring, and always there for my siblings Tom and Carol and me. She taught us to be responsible, independent, and the best that we could be. Education was important to her. She had always wanted to go to college and become a teacher, but she knew that neither she nor her parents could afford it. After high school she did administrative work.

I always wanted to be a teacher from the time I was in kindergarten. My mother encouraged me to pursue that goal and I taught for thirty-three years, loving what I did every day. My mother also loved to be with her children and grandchildren as much as she could, so we spent a lot of time with her during the summer months. Throughout that summer, I couldn't help but notice that she was gaining weight in her stomach area and nowhere else. I asked her if she felt well and she replied "Yes," but that was her usual answer. When I noticed that the whites of her eyes were becoming pale yellow, I asked her again, to which she replied, "I'm fine." I suggested she have a check-up with her doctor, but she declined, even when I said I would go with her. By the end of the summer, she was slowing down physically, and I repeated that she needed to see her doctor. She assured me she was fine, and I knew I couldn't make her go. I wonder now if she knew she was ill and didn't want to face whatever was wrong with her.

Before we knew it, it was September and I was back to work teaching, so life was busy: teaching during the day, talking to my kids about their day, transporting them to their various sports and activities after school, making dinner, and doing schoolwork I needed to do in the evening. My husband and I had also started looking for land on which we wanted to build a house. We lived in a city with an airplane flight path over our small Cape-style home. If we were on the phone or watching TV, we would have to stop talking or pause the TV until the plane was gone. We used to say we could see the treads on the plane's tires! Our children were leaving our nest, so we decided to build a house in a more rural area. Life went on. I spoke with my mom on the phone and saw her frequently, such as at the kids' sports events. I was always close to my mom, so we enjoyed sharing our lives with each other.

And then 9/11 happened. It changed everyone forever. We were all on high alert. My parents had been talking about going to Las Vegas for several years and had finally planned a trip there. They gambled a little, only once or twice a year. They had never been to Las Vegas, and I think they wanted to experience the shows and what Las Vegas was all about. Mom loved to travel and enjoy life in general but usually had to convince my dad it would be fun. This time we were concerned about their safety, as this was shortly after 9/11. But they belonged to the World War II generation, and they insisted they'd be fine. So off they went!

We picked them up at the airport when they returned. When I saw my mom walk off the plane, I couldn't believe how sick she looked. She was walking so slowly. It looked like the trip had taken a lot out of her. She told me she was tired and needed to rest. A few days later I reiterated that she should have her doctor check her out and said I'd be happy to take a day off from school and go with her. She finally agreed to make an appointment, but she said I didn't need to go with her as my dad could always go with her if she needed someone. Even though she said that, I felt she'd probably just want to go by herself as she was always such an independent woman. I felt better now that she had agreed to see her doctor and I knew she'd get back to me with the results of her visit.

Time went on. Ken and I were getting excited because we were narrowing down the possibilities of which land to buy and what style of house to build. One day I woke up in bed and knew something was wrong. I felt like I had a dark cloud above me, a sense that something bad was going to happen today, something that would change my life forever. I didn't say anything to anyone, but the feeling lingered with me all day. My husband was commuting to Boston every day and I wondered if he would get into an accident, or if something might happen to our kids. I had one of the best days teaching in my classroom.

By the time I left school I thought, *This is weird, everything's fine,* but that dark cloud was still above me. I got home from school and asked my daughter how her day was. She said it was good and filled me in on the details. Then she returned to her bedroom upstairs. I started dinner and decided to block it out, since everything seemed to be going well.

A short time later my daughter appeared on the stairs and said, "Oh, Mom, I forgot to tell you that Grammy called and asked for you, but I told her you weren't home from school yet. She asked me to have you call her when you got home. And she didn't sound like Grammy."

My heart sank. I stopped preparing dinner and called my mom.

"I have cancer," she said, in a voice that didn't sound like hers. She told me that she had gone to see her doctor recently and he had sent her for some tests. Today someone from his office had called her and given her the results. I now understood why the dark cloud was above me all day. The next day it was gone.

Everything after that seemed like a dream, unreal. My mom, my dad, my brother and sister, and my husband and I met with a cancer specialist to discuss the diagnosis: stage 4, terminal, possibly six months to live. There would be no need to go through treatments. It was the end of October, and I was getting ready for parent-teacher conferences in early November. I talked to my husband and told him that after my conferences were over, I wanted to take a leave of absence and spend as much time as I could with my mom. He said that whatever I wanted to do was fine with him.

The Sunday before conferences, my husband and I went to visit my mom and dad. I told her that we had put a deposit down on a piece of land that already had the foundation laid for the style of the house we wanted to build, and we'd like to take her to see it. As she sat on her couch in her nightgown and bathrobe, she told me that she didn't think she had the energy to get dressed. I told her I would help her, but if she didn't want to go that was fine with me. She slowly got up and I helped her get dressed. When we got there, I walked down the driveway with her. We looked at the foundation and land, but within a few minutes she said she was too tired and needed to go back to the car. She and I walked slowly back to the car and sat there while Ken and my dad explored a little bit. We talked a little and sat quietly together. For some reason I was so grateful that my mom would know where I was going to be living in the future.

A few days later I had a full day of school and parent-teacher conferences scheduled until well into the evening. In the middle of the afternoon my principal, Anita, came to me and said my aunt had called and I needed to go to my mom's immediately.

I looked at her and said, "What about all my conferences? Parents will be coming, and I won't be here."

"Give me your list and I will call them all and let them know that when you get back you will call them to reschedule," she said. (She was a blessing!)

My mom was now in a coma. We were all with her for the next couple of days. The hospice nurse kept asking me if there was someone my mom hadn't seen or talked to yet, someone she may be waiting for. I said, no, all the kids and grandkids had come and her siblings who couldn't come had spoken with her by phone.

My oldest son, Derek, remembered that my mom's favorite Christmas present was a calendar for the new year with all her grandchildren's pictures on it. He decided to get all seven of them together. They went to a photographer that Friday and had a group picture of them taken. He came back with a wallet size. I was so surprised that they had done this. One of my nieces, Melinda, put it in my mom's hand, and my dad and I told her it was okay for her to go to be with her mother and family and God. We would miss her every day, but we wanted her to be happy and not sick. She passed away a short time later that same day.

I had assumed that if I had a possible six months with my mother, I could easily take a few weeks to complete conferences and then spend time with her. That was a wakeup call that things don't always happen the way we expect them to. Life doesn't always happen the way we plan it. Life happens on its own terms. I never got to take a leave of absence and spend more time with her, since she passed away about one month after her diagnosis. This is the biggest regret of my life, but I am so thankful that I had spent so much time with her during my life. My advice to others: don't wait, spend time, pick up the phone and call, as you may not be able to tomorrow.

Chapter 4

Dad's Not Here

I was teaching in my classroom on a Friday in March when our school secretary came in to tell me there was a fireman on the phone who wanted to talk to me. He was at my dad's house. She stayed with my class as I hurried to the office. The fireman told me that my Aunt Claire had found my dad on his kitchen floor. I asked if my dad was alert and the fireman said yes, he was alert and seemed to understand when they talked to him. The fireman also asked if I could meet them at the hospital. What he didn't tell me was that my dad wasn't able to speak.

When my husband and I got to the hospital, the doctor in the emergency room said that he had told my dad that he was going to ask him some questions. If the answer was "yes," the doctor wanted him to raise one finger, and if it was "no" he should raise two fingers. The doctor said that my dad could definitely comprehend what he was saying; he had answered all questions correctly. They would need to do some tests, but it looked like he'd had a stroke. I had been talking to my dad, but when he heard that the doctor thought he'd had a stroke he turned to me and raised two fingers. I knew what he meant: he did not want to be put on life support. I told him I understood but that we'd have to see what the tests showed. If there was any hope that he could recover, we wanted to know. My father had seen his brother-in-law, my Uncle Jay, who'd had a massive stroke and couldn't talk or walk, live in that state for about five years. My dad had sternly told me that if that ever happened to him, he did not want to be put on life support. He had made me promise that I wouldn't do that and had put this wish in his living will.

By Sunday the tests were completed and two of the doctors met with my sister, my brother, my husband, and me. They told us there was absolutely no hope for recovery, since he'd had a massive stroke at the base of his brain stem. We looked at each other and started to cry. We knew what we had to do. They had put him on life support while they were doing all the tests. We all agreed that we had to take him off life support. It was the most difficult thing I've ever had to do. We called close family and friends to come to say their goodbyes, since that afternoon they would be taking him off life support.

We had been told that he could pass away in a few hours or live for several days, so we all stayed at the hospital until about four o'clock the next morning. At that point we decided that it would be better to go home, get some sleep, shower, and then come back. My brother stayed every night and the rest of us were with my father during the day and evening. We would stand by his bed and talk to him and make him more comfortable. I got used to his breathing patterns. When we were talking to him, his breathing would speed up; sometimes I felt that he was trying to talk back to us.

One night, I think it was Wednesday, my sister was standing on the left side of his bed, and I was standing on the right side. His breathing was slow and steady. Even when we spoke directly to him, it remained the same. Something was different. I felt like he wasn't there with us.

I finally looked at my sister and said, "He's not here."

My sister looked at me and said, "What are you talking about?"

I said, "I know it sounds odd, but I feel like his body is here, but his spirit might be in transition between here and Heaven."

She and I talked a little more, and when she left, I decided to walk the hospital halls. It was so quiet I thought I could just walk and think about what I was feeling that night.

As I passed the nurse's station, the only nurse there came around the desk and approached me, saying, "Are you okay? How's everything going?"

I looked at her and said, "If I told you, you'd think I was crazy."

She smiled and said, "No, I've heard it all, trust me."

So, I told her that I thought my dad's spirit might be in transition, as his body was resting so peacefully with no response to anything. I just didn't feel like he was there with us. "Have you ever heard of anything like that?"

She said, "Yes, actually, I have."

"Do you think I'm crazy?" I asked.

"No, I don't. Who's to say?" she replied.

I thanked her for listening and she said that that was what she was there for. The next night, Thursday, my sister and I were back at my dad's bedside. I touched his hand and started talking to him and his breathing quickened.

I looked up at my sister and said, "He's back."

She looked at me and said, "You're starting to scare me."

I said, "I feel like his spirit is here now, but it wasn't last night."

Later on, I had a chance to talk to the same nurse as the previous night. I told her that I felt he was back, and she smiled.

Again, I said, "Am I crazy?"

And she said again, "No, I've had other people tell me things like that. Who's to know?"

To this day I don't know why his spirit would go away and then return. The doctors had him on medication to keep him comfortable. The only reason I can think of for him to want to stay would be so he could be near his family, since at least one of us was with him at all times. As I mentioned previously, my brother, Tom, slept in the next room every night. My sister, Carol, my dad's sister, Claire, my cousin, Linda, my husband Ken and I, and others came during the day or evening.

We couldn't understand how my dad could still be with us. When we spoke to the doctors, they said that his heart was very strong and that sometimes this happened. On Friday night, a week later, after leaving the hospital, I fell asleep on the couch at home. At 12:55 a.m., early on Saturday morning, I woke up with a start. I was surprised to wake up so suddenly. I decided to go into the kitchen and empty the dishwasher and then go upstairs to bed. But about five to ten minutes later my phone rang, and my brother told me that my dad had just passed away. I asked what time it had been, and he said 12:55 a.m. The nurse had woken my brother just before that, since she thought it might be soon and he might want to be with him.

I called my sister to tell her of our dad's passing and she answered right away. She had woken up at 12:55 a.m., also. Sometime later, my close cousin, Linda, who is like an older sister to me, told me that she had woken up at 12:55 a.m., also. I couldn't help but wonder if Dad was "making the rounds" (as he used to say when he visited others) to visit with us before he continued on his journey. I miss him and my mom so much, but I am so happy that they are finally at peace together.

Chapter 5

Thank You

A short while after my dad had passed away, I was in my kitchen and realized I could feel his presence, like his spirit was nearby. I smiled and looked around and thought, *I know you're here, Dad, I can feel your presence. It's comforting, actually. I miss you so much, but we're okay if you're checking in on us.* And then I thought, *People would think I'm strange, but I can feel his spirit is here with us for some reason.* I didn't say anything to my husband; I didn't know what he would think.

The next day I felt the same way—my father's spirit was still there in our house. I smiled and went about my day, but I couldn't help but wonder why he was still there.

On the third day, my husband had gone downstairs to the basement to work at his workbench. After about a half hour, I heard him come back up the stairs and open the door to the kitchen. I looked up from what I was doing and looked at him.

When I saw his face I asked, "Are you alright? Is everything okay?"

Ken looked pale. He walked into the kitchen and said, "You're not going to believe what just happened."

"What?" I asked, thinking maybe he had hurt himself, even though he looked fine.

"I was working at my workbench, and I felt a hand on my shoulder. I thought it was you, so I said, 'Did you come down here to bother me?' When you didn't answer, I turned around and no one was there. I felt a hand, a heavy strong hand, on my shoulder."

I started to smile. He just looked at me.

"It was my dad," I said.

My dad had worked on the railroad, as I've mentioned, and he had also been a labor foreman for Davison Construction. He had done construction work most of his life. That's all I remember him doing during my lifetime.

"This is the third day I've felt his presence in our house, and I've been wondering why he's been here," I told my husband. "I think I know now. He wants to thank you for helping me with everything that we've needed to do since he passed away. He knows that with your help, everything was a lot easier for me. I also think he wanted to come to you when you were alone. He was probably comfortable coming to you when you were at your workbench. Do you think I'm crazy?"

"No," Ken said thoughtfully. "It was definitely a strong man's hand."

"And I know," I replied, "that he would be so thankful for all the help you've given me. I also know that in his life he was always helping other people, so usually they were the ones thanking him rather than the other way around."

The next day, I woke up and my dad's spirit was gone. I was sad, but I knew he was at peace now. He had accomplished what he came by to do. But every once in a while, I do feel like my dad, my mom, or someone close to me is nearby or looking down on us. I do believe that we have angels looking out for us. And I find that comforting!

Chapter 6

Pa Sends a Message

One Sunday morning I was taking a shower and getting ready to go to church. Because I was in the shower, I didn't hear the phone ring. After I dressed and grabbed my purse (I had a tendency to be late for church), my husband and I got in the car and headed off. After Mass, as we drove home and were talking, my husband said, "Oh, I forgot to tell you that Julia called this morning and said she needed to talk to you, but you were in the shower. I told her that we were getting ready to go to church and I'd let you know so you could call her back when we get home."

"That's odd that she would call so early in the morning," I replied. "I hope nothing's wrong. How did she sound? Did she say anything else?"

"She did sound anxious to talk to you," he said. "She wanted to tell you about an experience that she had last night. She seemed disappointed that you weren't able to talk to her right then."

My niece Julia and I talk frequently on the phone; she lives on the West Coast, and I live on the East Coast. Julia is my brother Tom's daughter. She'd never called me so early in the morning, though. I couldn't wait to get home to call her. It was the first thing I did when I walked through the door. As I picked up the phone to call her, I was hoping that nothing was wrong and that she was alright.

When she answered, she said excitedly, but seriously, "Aunt Lu, I wanted to call you last night, but it was very late, so I didn't want to wake you up."

"You know you can call me any time," I replied.

"I know, but I decided to wait until morning," she said. "You won't believe what happened last night. I went to a birthday dinner for one of my friends. The only person I knew at this dinner was the birthday girl, whom I was sitting next to. I had just got back from Pa's funeral on the East Coast, and no one there had known about Pa passing away. We were all sitting at a long table. As we were talking with others around us, I noticed a lady at the far end of the table looking at me. Every once in a while, she would continue to glance over at me. It was starting to make me uncomfortable. Suddenly, she got up and started to walk towards me. She sat down next to me and told me that she 'had a strong sense that she got from me.' She explained that she was a medium and that she could connect with spirits. She explained that my Pa had something to tell me. I knew exactly who it was because I only had one 'Pa.'"

My niece and I have a special relationship. She and I share spiritual events that have happened in our lives with each other. Julia shared the following spiritual event with me: "She said this man is telling me, 'My partner in crime was taken from me.'"

Julia and my dad ("Pa," as she called him, her grandfather) always had a special bond. Sometimes they would joke that they were "partners in crime," because when the two of them were together others would joke that they were up to something. They had the same type of humor and liked to get a rise out of everyone. My dad loved her fun-loving, happy personality and she loved to "get him going" or tease him.

Julia told me that she didn't say a word, just continued to listen to this lady.

I interrupted her by saying, "Julia, are you sure you hadn't told your friends about your grandfather passing away?"

"No, I haven't told anyone, Aunt Lu," she replied.

"Had you talked to your friends about Grandpa?" I asked.

"No, why would I talk to my friends about Pa?"

"Okay, I just wanted to make sure," I replied.

This lady told Julia that this man was now telling her that he wanted her to tell Julia the following exact words: "He knew what was going on at the time. He did hurt for a short time but was gone very quickly thereafter. He wants everyone to know he did not suffer and is much happier now gambling with the best of them."

I started to cry.

"That was for me," I said. "I've worried and wondered if he had suffered from the time he had the stroke on a Friday to the next Friday when he passed away." I felt such a relief to know he hadn't.

Did I think he was gambling? No, I don't, but who am I to say? I do think he would say that so we would know it was him, since he liked to go to Foxwoods once in a while. Julia told me that she used to call him frequently. She lived on the opposite side of the country from him and liked to check in with him. He would always tell her when he went on a bus trip to the casino. Julia told me that as he got older, she liked that he did those group trips because it gave them something to talk about. At the same time, Julia was taking some trips to Vegas with her friends. Each time, she would call him a day or two beforehand, on her way, or while she was there. She would make a point to ask him what to bet on, black or red. Julia told me it was their little inside joke, and they did it each trip.

Julia continued, "The lady at the dinner also told me that 'he is proud of everyone. Although he's stubborn, he knows he has the best family, the best-looking bunch.'"

My dad expected a lot from his children. He would tell you when he thought you were doing something wrong and what you should be doing instead. He didn't give praise for anything unless it was earned. Listening to Julia, I felt like he was finally telling us how proud he was of us. He wanted us to know he loved his family, which of course, we already knew, since he was always there to help anyone if they needed it. When the seven cousins, my dad's seven grandchildren, would take pictures together and someone would have that picture in hand, my dad would say, "Now, that's a good-lookin' bunch!"

I do believe that people who have passed on can connect with people here on Earth. I have felt the presence of God, my parents, and others. I do believe they find ways to send messages to us. However, I am a "doubting Thomas" and want to make sure that the people who claim to be intermediaries are genuine. From what this woman told my niece, I can't imagine how anyone would know all of those things, especially the exact words that he wanted her to say. That does sound like my father, though, making sure she was saying what he asked her to say so we would know it was really him.

I thought about all of this for a long time. One thing that bothered me was, why did he not come to me? Why did he go to Julia? After I thought about it, I realized that of course he would connect with Julia, as they had a special relationship. He found ways to reach Julia and she was the conduit to me. I had a great relationship with him, but they were definitely "partners in crime."

Chapter 7

Love Around the Table

During the COVID pandemic, Julia had a chance to see an energy healer. Right away the practitioner said, "Do you know a Gerald or Jerry that has passed?" (As I mentioned earlier, my dad's name was Gerald, but most people called him Jerry.) "His energy is coming in very strong. You both had a lot in common: your minds are sharp and you both don't like stupid people."

She continued, "He has an ego thing going on; who I am seeing him as is someone that is a lot younger than when he passed, or what you are remembering him as. He is saying you would have remembered him as an old worn-out tire and that is not how he is coming across now. A young guy, *hot!*"

Julia said this made her laugh because Pa would always tell her how he was a hot young stud and describe how good-looking he was, especially in his Army uniform. When she told me this, I started to laugh because he was a handsome man. He was proud to have served his country. A picture of him in his uniform hung on the wall in my childhood home.

The practitioner continued to say, "He also is patting someone on the back, saying, 'My good ol' boy, Tommy.'"

His best friend, Tommy, had passed away three years after my dad.

She then said, "Dorothy or Doris . . . he is saying that they are all hanging out with Rachel, sitting around the table . . . I think he just wants you to know that you have a lot of love around you."

As I mentioned earlier, my dad's mom was named Doria and some people called her Doris. Rachel was my mother's name. When people came to visit, we would all gather around the kitchen table. Even with, or especially because of, all the lively, contentious discussions, there was definitely a lot of love!

I was shocked when Julia told me about her visit to this energy healer. In the past I have been skeptical about what people have been told from mediums and the like. Sometimes it seems like the information they share is too general and could apply to other people as well. However, this one was extremely accurate not only with the names of my dad, his best friend, my grandmother, and my mother, but also with the personality of my dad. Also, this was the first time that my dad had mentioned my mom and my grandmother. I was ecstatic to hear their names mentioned! I was also so happy to hear that they were all together. It was very comforting.

Chapter 8

A Special Bond

One night when Julia was working at a steakhouse, she had a feeling that one of the guests was staring at her for a while. When she came back to the table with their drinks, this person continued to stare at her.

Finally, the person just blurted out, "You need to call your favorite aunt."

Julia laughed and said, "Okay, yeah, sure."

This person continued to tell Julia that she was a medium. She told her that she knew that she and this aunt were close.

Ever since Julia was little, she used to joke with me that she was my favorite niece. She still does this mostly because she likes to joke and stir the pot in a playful way, especially when my other two nieces, Crystal and Melinda, are around. Julia and I have always known that we have a close bond. And, of course, I do love them all!

Julia had not called me for a while, longer than we usually go, so she did call me after the medium had spoken to her. When Julia calls, she always asks how Ken and I are doing and what we've been up to. It was summertime. I told her that I went into our pool to swim (my favorite sport) and the more I swam the more pain I had. She asked if I had been to a doctor. I said yes, and told Julia that my doctor thought I had sciatica. We continued our discussion about that and a few other things. She continued to call once in a while to check on me. I hadn't called to tell Julia about the pain that I was having, as I knew she would have worried about me. It's interesting that the medium knew we were close and that she felt that Julia needed to call me.

The medium had also said that "It would be a great time."

Julia and her brother, Jordan, had been planning a surprise fortieth wedding anniversary party for their parents—my brother and his wife, Colleen—for about the last nine months. In the beginning of their planning, Julia had asked if I would help them. I said I would, but I didn't know how I could help as I lived so far away. She said the most important thing she needed help with was getting her parents to the party without them knowing about it. She wanted them to be surprised.

Ken and I talked about it and came up with a plan. We suggested taking them to a national park and doing some walking and exploring. If we had more time, we were going to stop in at some local wineries in the area for wine tasting. Unfortunately, on the day of the party we never got to do the wine tasting; Julia texted me to let me know that everyone was at the party waiting for us. I made up an excuse and we drove to the party. Tom and Colleen were so surprised! It was clear that they had never suspected to be celebrating their fortieth wedding anniversary that day. It was a wonderful party with family and friends, some they hadn't seen in quite a while. Julia and I have wondered if the fortieth wedding anniversary party could have been what the medium was referring to when she said, "It would be a great time."

I don't know why mediums seem to be drawn to Julia, but two possible reasons come to mind. One is because that's what mediums do. They receive messages from spirits (people who have passed away) and then pass the messages on to the people they are intended for. The other reason is that several of the messages from mediums for Julia have been from my dad. He can be persistent, and he had messages that he felt were important for his family to hear. For whatever reason, I'm glad that we have some connection to our loved ones who have passed away.

Chapter 9

In His Time

Trust and have faith in God. How can you trust in someone you can't see? It's easy to trust in someone you can see. I have found that once I started "talking" to God and developing a relationship with Him, I could feel His presence with me. It is comforting to feel God's presence. When I "talk" to God, whether it be to discuss a problem with which I need help or guidance, or for any other reason, I have found that He finds a way to let me know which path I should take. If I listen to Him and take that path, it always ends up being the best one.

The following story is one example of this.

There is a place not far from my home that is called the Precious Blood Monastery. There is a little chapel there where people go to pray and light candles. I go occasionally, as it is a peaceful, quiet place to sit and pray, reflect, and talk to God. One day when I got up to leave, I noticed a woman named Dorothy, or Dot, as we called her, coming down the side aisle. She had been a friend of my parents. I waited for her at the back of the chapel. We greeted each other and decided to go through the first set of doors into the lobby area to talk. As we were talking, Dot asked me how things were going. I told her that my oldest son, Derek, had discovered a lump that was cancerous and had undergone surgery to remove it. Six months later it was showing signs that it might be coming back, so he and his doctors decided to do radiation. And now, I told her, he was cancer free!

While I was telling her all this, a middle-aged woman had come out of the chapel, walked through the lobby, and gone out through the second set of doors. A minute or so later, she came back in and walked over to me. She held out a beautiful crucifix on a chain and told me that she wanted me to have it.

I was speechless, but then thinking that she had overheard my conversation with my friend, I said, "Oh, no, my son is fine, he's cancer free."

She repeated that she still wanted me to have it.

I said, "It's beautiful, I've never seen anything like it before."

She said, "It's an exact duplicate of what the Pope wears. I got it when I was in Italy."

To which I said, "Oh, I can't possibly take this. You need to keep it."

She said, "You don't understand." Using her index finger, she pointed upward, saying, "He is telling me to give this to you, not me. He insists I give this to you, so that's what I have to do."

She then reached out to put it in my hands.

I didn't know what to say, but finally said, "Thank you so much!"

She smiled, turned around, and walked out the door.

I turned to Dot and said, "What just happened?"

Dot smiled at me and said, "You can't argue with that."

The two of us said a few more words to each other as we walked outside, said goodbye to each other, and went to our cars. I sat in my car, and I thought, *God, I'm okay now. My son is cancer free. Why are you giving this to me now?* Silence. Then I actually felt a little angry. *I don't understand, God. Why didn't you give this to me when my son was going through everything? Why*

*now?! I could have used it a year ago. Now I feel like a weight has
been lifted from my shoulders.*

Suddenly, I realized I was chastising God! And I certainly
didn't want to do that. I calmed down and thought, *I just don't
understand, God.*

All of a sudden, I heard a voice in my head (that's the only
way I can describe it) that I'd never heard before. The voice said,
"Now you give this to your son." *Oh, my gosh,* I thought. *Does
my son need this? But is he going to think I'm crazy if I tell him
what happened today?* I also thought, like the woman who gave
this crucifix to me, that I didn't have a choice. That was what
God wanted and that was what I would do. I apologized to
God about how angry I had gotten and let him know that I
would give it to my son.

When I got home, my husband looked at me and said, "Are
you okay? Has something happened?"

I said, "You're going to think I'm crazy."

"No," he said, "I won't think you're crazy."

I proceeded to tell him what had happened.

He listened intently, then asked, "What are you going to do?"

I said, "Our son is going to think I'm crazy, but I have to
give it to him."

I waited for an opportune time to give it to him. During the
next few days, I started to wonder: *Why would he need it now?
He had told me he was cancer free. Is there something he isn't telling
me?* A few days later I was babysitting his two boys and we were
going to meet at a designated place so he could take the boys
home with him. When we met up, the boys put their things in
their car and hopped in. I asked Derek if I could talk to him
for a few minutes. He said sure. I told him I hoped he wouldn't

think I was crazy, but . . . Then I proceeded to tell him the story of what happened.

He listened intently and when I was finished, I said, "Do you think I'm crazy?"

He said, "No."

I said, "Do you want this?"

I held out the crucifix on the chain.

He said, "Yes."

I was so happy.

I don't like to pry into my adult children's lives, so I couldn't bring myself to ask him why he wanted it. There could be many reasons, but I didn't ask until many years later. When I finally asked him, he said there were several reasons. He had been brought up going to church every Sunday and even though he may not go now, that didn't mean he didn't have a strong faith in God. His experience with cancer was another reason why he accepted this beautiful crucifix. He told me that if the person felt compelled to give it to me and then I chose to give it to him, then who was he to object if in fact a higher power was in play?

He also felt that when people get sick, like he had with his cancer, and were in states where they were weaker or more vulnerable, they often sought help in a variety of places, such as science, religion, relationships, and so forth, for help, guidance, and healing. I, and I'm sure many other people, could certainly identify with that. Also, because it was an object or relic, it had permanence, and oftentimes that makes things more "real." He also said he accepted it because it was from me.

Looking back now I realize God was with us from my son's diagnosis, through his treatments, to our current time. And I believe he will continue to be with us always, even if He is silent.

Chapter 10

A Nighttime Visitor

After I wrote the previous chapter, which included my son, Derek, I remembered another time when Derek had an experience that we still can't completely understand. He was much younger when he had this experience. Actually, it has been over three decades since it happened. I'm glad I remembered this one, since it's relevant to all of the experiences that I've had or have been connected to.

After Ken and I got married, we lived in an apartment on the second floor. We had our first son, Derek, a little over a year after we got married. Sixteen months later we had our second son, Brad. They grew up together playing baseball and soccer, and many times having the same friends. About three months before Derek's fifth birthday, we moved from an apartment to a small Cape-style house. In the apartment the boys had slept in bunk beds on the same floor as our bedroom. However, in the house, they now slept on the second floor, and we slept on the first floor.

The boys shared a tiny bedroom. When you stood in the doorway and looked to your left, you would see the side of Brad's bureau with its back against the wall by your left arm. If you looked to your right, you would see the side of Derek's bureau with its back against the wall by your right arm. There was about two feet between their bureaus and the foot of their twin beds. The room was about eleven feet by twelve feet.

The boys had a small TV on Brad's bureau. When the Nintendo Entertainment System came out, they were both excited to get one. They loved sitting on their beds to watch TV or standing right in front of the TV to play Nintendo. Occasionally they'd stay up way past their bedtime doing that.

One night, when Derek was about nine years old, he woke up in the middle of the night, around two o'clock. He sat up in bed and saw a boy standing in the doorway, only six feet away from him. Everything was calm. He looked across the room to where Brad was sleeping. He now knew that the boy in the doorway was not Brad.

A day or two later, when he told me about this, he said he remembered saying, "Okay," as he wasn't worried or concerned. Even though everything was calm, he told me that he'd been nervous because of what he was looking at, so he lay back down, pulled the sheet over his head, and waited for a little while. When he pulled the sheet back down, the boy was gone.

I remember when he told me about this happening, I listened intensely because I knew he was telling me the truth about what had happened and what he had seen. I did ask him if it could have been a dream, to which he replied no, he had sat up in his bed and was awake. I thought about this for a little while.

The family next door to us were great neighbors: Priscilla, Paul, and their five children. We became close friends. They had lived in their house for many years. Priscilla knew most of the people in the neighborhood and what was going on. I decided to talk to her, but I didn't say anything about Derek seeing a boy in his bedroom doorway in the middle of the night.

One day when I had the opportunity to talk to her alone, I asked her how many families had lived in our house prior to us living there. She said there had been two families before us. I asked her if either family had children.

She said, "Yes, why do you want to know?"

"Oh, I was just curious about who had lived in our house before us," I replied, which was true. I then asked her my last and most important question: "Did they have a son?"

Priscilla replied, "Yes, a little boy and a younger girl. It was so sad, though. When they left here they moved to Florida, and the little boy died there."

My heart went out to that family; I couldn't imagine losing a child. I couldn't help but wonder if this was the little boy that Derek had seen. Could he have returned to the house that he'd once lived in? Did he want to see who was living in his house or maybe, especially, who was now in his bedroom? We may never know, but maybe someday we'll find out.

Chapter 11

The Little Silver Angel

I always felt like I had the best mother-in-law in the world! Cecile welcomed me from the first day I met her, in the spring of my senior year in high school. Ken had told his parents a little bit about me. Cecile and Louis invited me into their home with smiles on their faces. They were very pleasant. We talked for a little while and then Ken and I left on our date.

When Ken got home later that evening, his mom said, "Lucy seems very nice. She doesn't look like she's Puerto Rican."

Ken was a little puzzled and then said, "I didn't say she is Puerto Rican. I said she is Portuguese."

And that was the beginning of my relationship with Cecile! She didn't care what nationality I was. She welcomed me wholeheartedly. She never judged, criticized, or interfered in our family life in any way. She and my father-in-law, Louis, were always loving, caring, and helpful in many, many ways. They both worked very hard. My mother-in-law worked in several textile mills, including Manchester Hosiery Mill, Stevens Mill, and Velcro USA. She liked working the second or third shifts so she could be with her children, Ken and Betty. She could also get shopping, or whatever she needed to do, done during the day.

My father-in-law worked in the horse barn at Blake's Creamery when he was a young teenager. Milk was delivered to homes and businesses using horse drawn wagons. When he became eighteen years old and a junior in high school, he was drafted into the US Army during World War II. He originally served in Africa and then was part of the invasion of Italy. As he had a deep knowledge of working with harnesses, he was assigned to the Eighty-Eighth Division's Headquarters Company in their Pioneer and Engineering unit. His two main functions were mine detection and leading mules loaded with supplies. I recall stories he told like probing for mines with his bayonet at night, being shot at when sweeping for mines, or being shown a map (that he could not keep and had to memorize) and then leading a train of mules at night into the mountains to the front lines with supplies, and having to be back before daylight.

When he was seventy-nine years old, Louis received his Bronze Star. A reporter asked him why he didn't get it at the end of the war.

My father-in-law explained, "You don't understand that during World War II, everyone was somehow involved in or impacted by the war. When the war ended, we just wanted to get home!"

Shortly after returning home from the war, the owner of Blake's Creamery asked my father-in-law if he would work a couple of weeks delivering milk to stores, since one of the drivers needed some time off. He would start his day around four o'clock in the morning. The two weeks turned into months, and then into years. My father-in-law retired after having worked for Blake's for fifty years.

Even though they had busy weeks, my in-laws still found time to prepare delicious Sunday dinners. Cecile loved to cook and bake for people, and she was excellent at both. In the summer, when Cecile and Louis had vacation time, they loved to take our children to amusement parks, babysit them when needed, and help us in any way they could.

My father-in-law had been skilled in woodworking since he was in high school. In high school he made his own table saw. When Ken and I were engaged and shopping for bedroom furniture, we came back to his parents' house a little discouraged. We had found a bureau that I liked, but it would be too large for an apartment. Louis asked us if we had found anything. We explained the situation to him. He went over to a kitchen drawer, opened it, and picked up his tape measure.

"Let's take a ride and you can show me what it looks like."

We got in our car and drove to the furniture store and showed him the bureau that I liked. He asked me what size I wanted and then proceeded to take some measurements in preparation to make his own version. He didn't have a pad or pencil. He kept all the measurements in his head. He ended up making us the bureau, Ken's armoire dresser, a nightstand, our bed, and a frame for a large wall mirror. As our family grew, he went on to make a baby cradle, a crib, a sewing machine cabinet, our children's twin beds, and many other pieces of furniture for us and others. He was an intelligent person in many ways who enjoyed and shared his hobby by helping others.

After my father-in-law passed away and my mother-in-law grew older, she developed what she referred to as "a bad knee." She could walk but it was difficult for her, and she didn't want to use a cane or a walker, even though she eventually used both.

Then, one evening in January 2016, Cecile had a stroke. She was ninety-one years old. She was quickly admitted to the ER. With a video link to a specialist at Mass General Hospital in Boston, the specialist determined that she was a candidate for the tPA drug to minimize the effect of the stroke by dissolving blood clots. The drug was administered through a vein in her arm within the first three hours to be most effective. She was hospitalized for a few days. Now she could no longer walk on her own. However, she could talk, participate in conversations, read, and use her arms and hands. Because she was not able to walk on her own, she was placed in a skilled nursing home.

This skilled nursing home provided physical therapy, occupational therapy, speech therapy, and so forth for patients who need to regain their mobility and speech to reclaim some of their independence. Eventually, this became her new home. This facility was only about ten minutes from our house. My husband was still working, but I had recently retired so I was able to visit with her daily and my husband would visit after work and weekends. After my mother's terminal cancer diagnosis and her passing within a month when she had been given up to six months to live, I didn't want to take any chance that I would make the same mistake again. I wanted to spend as much time as I could with my mother-in-law, whom I loved dearly.

Cecile loved it when her children, grandchildren, and great-grandchildren came to visit her. Her great-grandchildren loved to put together puzzles and play games with her.

My husband and I noticed that his mom had a wonderful long-term memory. She would tell us lots of stories about when she was growing up as a child but seemed to have difficulty with more recent events. One day when we visited her, I was shocked when she quietly asked me if she had a husband. My heart broke!

I looked at Ken and then turned back to her and said, "Yes, remember, Mom, he liked to go fishing. He also loved working in his garden."

My husband and I continued to tell her a few more things that Louis had liked to do and that they had done together.

When we left that day, I told my husband that I was going to make a book for her. It would be simple. Each page would have a picture of a person or people (her husband, his brother Jay, who was his fishing buddy, a grandchild, and so forth). Under their photo would be one or two sentences that told her who that person was and something about that person.

When I completed the book, my husband and I went to visit my mother-in-law. I told Mom that I had something for her and handed her the book. I said, "Let's look at it together."

As we went through each page, we discussed each picture.

"Where did you buy this?" she asked.

"I didn't buy it, Mom," I explained. "I made this for you."

"You made this?" she asked.

"Yes," I replied.

When we got to the end, Cecile went to hand the book back to me.

I said, "Oh, no, Mom, this is for you to keep."

Her face lit up and she said, "It's mine?"

"Yes," I replied, "I made it for you."

"Thank you!" she said with a big smile on her face.

When we went back to visit her on other days, the staff would tell us that she would look through the book every day and show it to anyone who walked into her room. I was so happy seeing how happy she was. I wanted to make sure that she wouldn't forget the people she loved, especially her wonderful husband.

A little over a year after she had entered the nursing home, her older sister, Yvonne, became a resident of the facility too.

The two of them loved to meet in the large family gathering rooms or in each other's room to talk. They were both hard of hearing, but they enjoyed their time together very much. At times, it made for some interesting conversations.

In September 2018, my mother-in-law's sister passed away. The day after her passing, my husband and I went to visit his mom. As her memory was failing, we decided it was best not to tell her that her sister had passed away, as she would have been heartbroken, and the next day she would ask about her again and then be heartbroken again. We didn't want this sad cycle to continue.

When we entered her room, my husband noticed something under Mom's wheelchair. He bent down and picked up a small silver angel charm. He couldn't believe it: an angel the day after losing her sister. We asked the nursing staff if anyone had lost a charm. No one had. We asked if she had had any visitors and that answer was no, also. Where did it come from? A short time later my husband's cousin Ruth stopped in to visit, as she was picking up her mother's belongings. When we showed her the angel, she had chills. We asked her if she recognized it. She hadn't seen it before and didn't know where it could have come from.

We'll never know where the small silver angel charm came from or how it appeared under my mother-in-law's chair . . . another mysterious unknown.

Chapter 12

Do It Myself or Trust in God?

One summer when I had an extremely painful back issue, I kept trying different things to get rid of the pain: ice, heat, meds, physical therapy. The pain was excruciating and constant. Even when I got a cortisone shot, it didn't relieve the pain.

I was getting so worn down and depressed after having constant pain for so long. It was almost three months, the whole summer, of trying to fix everything myself. I'm a person who likes to take control of my life and do everything myself. I love to swim and kayak, and I felt like I hadn't had a summer. Yes, I had asked God to help me get well, but I was still trying to fix this myself. It was difficult to do when I was in so much pain. I wondered why God wasn't helping me. I was getting frustrated. How could you be brave and strong and have a strong faith when you felt like God wasn't helping you?

It's difficult to trust God when you're going through hard times. But after many weeks of constant, intense pain, I decided to do just that. I finally realized that it didn't make much sense to only trust God when everything in my life was going well. I needed to trust Him when things weren't going well and I needed Him the most. So, one morning after I tried and succeeded, with difficulty and pain, to sit up on the edge of my bed, I finally decided to ask God earnestly to help me get well and that I would hand everything over to him. I would trust Him 100 percent and be confident that He would help me. When I sincerely trusted Him, everything started changing for the better. I continued to pray earnestly and trusted God wholeheartedly. I went to a specialist, got an MRI, and discovered I had a bulging disc. The next cortisone shot in that exact area helped tremendously. And with aquatic physical therapy, I was on the road to recovery.

One thing I do know is that God loves us. We are His children. He wants us to be happy. I believe that God wants us to pray to Him and ask Him for help and guidance. This was a difficult realization for me. I like to make my own decisions. I was brought up hearing "God helps those who help themselves." That may be, but Jesus helped the sick, the poor, and those who couldn't help themselves. And I discovered that when I ask God for help or guidance things work out much better, and everything seems to fall into place. God sees the whole picture and what's ahead. We can't do that.

However, God helps us in His time. He has reasons why He does things the way He does and when He does them. And it may take more time than we want it to. Sometimes we may wonder why it is taking so long for Him to answer our prayers. I know I have difficulty waiting for Him to answer me. I want things done now, while He may want to teach us something. Many times, I feel like He wants to teach me to have patience. But in my life, if I put things in His hands, the results are always better. God's timing, when I look back, is always better. And it helps to strengthen my faith in Him. Someday, hopefully, we will be able to ask Him all the questions that we've wanted answers to. I know I have a lot!

Epilogue

God works in mysterious ways. I have learned in my life that we don't always understand why things happen the way they do. And maybe we're not capable of that in this world. God, however, can see the whole picture, what's already happened, is currently happening, and what will happen in the future. Someday we will understand. In the meantime, we need to trust God, because He sees and knows all and can help us to make the best decisions, if we ask for His help.

Ever since I was a little girl, I could feel God's presence. It could be when I was out for a walk by myself, praying or talking to Him, or any time actually. Sometimes He would be silent, and I would wonder if He even heard me. But He always did, even if I didn't realize it until much later. Other times He would find a way to let me know which path He would want me to take. If I listened and took that path, it always turned out to be the best decision.

In the midst of our busy and sometimes chaotic lives, we just need to find a quiet place and be in God's presence . . . and listen. God is faithful and will not disappoint us. Don't lose hope. As the saying goes, "Keep the faith." My faith in God is what sustains me. Everything is easier in life with God by my side. And because God is loving and faithful and wants us to succeed and be happy, He has given us family and friends to support us. Keep the faith even in (and especially during) the toughest times. I have to continually remind myself of this, as it isn't easy, but I know from experience that it's the best thing to do.

God bless!

Acknowledgments

Thank you to God for always listening to me and guiding me. He was the one who encouraged me to write this spiritual memoir.

Thank you to my children, Derek, Brad, and Melissa, who are some of my first readers and editors and who have encouraged me on this journey.

Thank you to my grandchildren for their support, especially with marketing.

And thank you to my niece, Julia, for sharing her spiritual experiences with me.

About the Author

Lucy Geddes has always made books and storytelling a major part of her life, whether through teaching in the classroom for thirty-three years, reading to her children, or creating stories with her grandchildren. She and her husband live in New Hampshire, where she enjoys swimming, kayaking, biking, cross-country skiing, traveling, sewing, and of course, reading and writing. Lucy has also written and published three children's books: *Where Did Nicky Go?*, *Grammy Said, "NO!"*, and *What Is Grandpa Up to Now?*

In 2022, Lucy decided to try a different genre because there was another book that she wanted to write. She wanted to document all of the experiences that had happened in her life that she couldn't always explain or understand why they had happened. After thinking about them for many years, Lucy began to write them down. It took her about a year to write this book, a spiritual memoir that you are holding in your hands.

Please check out her website, LucyGeddesAuthor.com, where you will be able to read excerpts from her books and buy them directly. On this website you will also find bookstores in New Hampshire that carry Lucy's books. Listen to interviews and read reviews of her books as well. Enjoy reading!

9 798990 248410